Mississippi Valley Traveler
Small Town Pleasures
27 Small Mississippi River Towns For Day Trips and Long Weekends

by Dean Klinkenberg

Mysteries by Dean Klinkenberg:
Double-Dealing in Dubuque (Frank Dodge Mystery #2)
Rock Island Lines (Frank Dodge Mystery #1)

Guide Books by Dean Klinkenberg:
Lake Pepin Circle Tour
Headwaters Region Guide
Driftless Area Travel Guide
Lansing to LeClaire Travel Guide
Quad Cities Travel Guide

Watch for more books about the Mississippi River by the Mississippi Valley Traveler!

Find our more at:
www.MississippiValleyTraveler.com
www.DeanKlinkenberg.com

© Copyright 2017, 2018 by Dean Klinkenberg
Most recent update: November 2018

ISBN: 978-0-9908518-6-8

On the Cover: Fountain City, Wisconsin

CONTENTS

Introduction 6
Little Falls, Minnesota 8
Stockholm, Wisconsin 10
Pepin, Wisconsin 12
Lake City, Minnesota 14
Wabasha, Minnesota 16
Alma, Wisconsin 18
Fountain City, Wisconsin 20
Trempealeau, Wisconsin 22
Lansing, Iowa 24
Prairie du Chien, Wisconsin 26
Marquette & McGregor, Iowa 28
Guttenberg, Iowa 31
Potosi, Wisconsin 33
Galena, Illinois 35
Bellevue, Iowa 37
LeClaire, Iowa 39
Nauvoo, Illinois 41
Grafton, Illinois 44
Kimmswick, Missouri 46
Sainte Genevieve, Missouri 48
Chester, Illinois 50
New Madrid, Missouri 52
Rosedale, Mississippi 54
Lake Village, Arkansas 56
St. Francisville, Louisiana 58
Plaquemine, Louisiana 60
Donaldsonville, Louisiana 62

All photographs by Dean Klinkenberg, except:.

p. 58: Rosedown Plantation, St. Francisville, Louisiana; Rosedown Plantation-334 by Elisa.rolle, CC Attribution Share Alike 3.0

Back cover:

Tamales: Southern Foodways Alliance (https://commons.wikimedia.org/wiki/File:Tamale_Trail,_Helena-West_Helena,_AR_001.jpg); Creative Commons Attribution 2.0 Generic License

INTRODUCTION

Bellevue, Iowa

Big cities are great places to visit. Good food? There are hundreds of choices. Want to catch a show of some kind? No problem; pick an event. Sometimes, though, I get tired of the big city hassles, like sitting in traffic, waiting in long lines, or trying to figure out how to pay for an hour at the new parking meter.

Sometimes I just want to go to a place where the pace is slower, where I can leave my car behind and see the sights on foot. I want to visit a place where I can walk into a restaurant and get a table right away, where I can browse through a few antique shops at my own pace, where folks not only look me in the eye but are eager to strike up a conversation.

Those places are even more attractive to me if they come with great views of a major river, where I can take a leisurely stroll along the riverfront without dodging dozens of bicyclists, skateboarders, and joggers. There are times I just want to relax and watch the river roll by at a spot where I can hear birds chirping instead of cars honking.

Now that's a special place, at least for me. Lucky for me (and the rest of us), there are a couple dozen small towns along the Mississippi River where all this is possible, places that make for great diversions when we're looking for an alternative to a big city.

In fact, there are 27 small towns that fit the bill in my estimation; each one is described in this book. To be included on this list, each community had to have a population under 10,000 people (one has only 66 permanent residents!), and had to have enough going on to justify parking and walking around. While a half-day may be long enough to tour some of these towns, others will call out for a long weekend.

Small Mississippi River Towns

Most of these communities are located on the Upper Mississippi. There are a couple of reasons for this. The Mississippi's tendency to shift its channel hasn't been kind to towns on the lower river, swallowing a few and stranding others far from the river. In addition, the most interesting towns on the lower Mississippi tend to be small cities rather than small towns. Natchez, Mississippi, for example, is a great place to visit, but it has more than 10,000 residents.

Four of the towns in this book are on or near Lake Pepin, a natural lake in the main channel that was formed at the Mississippi's confluence with the Chippewa River. The drive around Lake Pepin is one of the most scenic anywhere along the Mississippi, which is that much more special because of these attractive small towns. Many people take a day to drive a loop around Lake Pepin, but a long weekend would be more rewarding. (If you're interested specifically in this area, check out my book called *Lake Pepin Circle Tour*.)

Use this book to get started, but most of all, get started. Take a walk along the river. Get a piece of pie. Find a tavern and share a drink with the folks who live there. Have a conversation. Above all, enjoy the slower pace. But be warned: this type of travel is terribly addictive.

You know you want some...(Blue Owl Bakery, Kimmswick, Missouri)

LITTLE FALLS, MINNESOTA
(8,343)

One of Frank Gosiak's murals

Little Falls is a picturesque small city that was built along the boundary where the forest and the prairie meet. Go west twenty miles and you'll be in farm country, but if you go twenty miles north, you'll be in thick forest. The Mississippi River passes over a series of small waterfalls that the Ojibwe Indians called Kakabikans (the little squarely cut off rock, or small falls). There was a prominent Ojibwe village nearby; it was home to the renowned leader Chief Pugon Geshig (also known as Hole-in-the-Day).

Europeans began moving into the area in the late 1840s. The falls provided an attractive source of power, so a dam and sawmill went up within a few years. Several sawmills opened in the latter part of the 19th century, especially after the hydroelectric power plant was completed in 1888. One of the biggest mills was the Pine Tree Lumber Company operated by Frederick Weyerhaeuser and Peter Musser. Little Falls was also the childhood home of famed aviator Charles Lindbergh and author Louise Erdrich.

The lumber mills are long gone (the pine forests were depleted a hundred years ago), but Little Falls has had a good base of light manufacturing, like Larson Boats, which has been in business since the 1920s.

What to Expect
Relaxing walks along the river, public art, and Lindbergh lore.

What to Visit

Charles Lindbergh grew up in a house on the banks of the Mississippi River. That house now hosts exhibits as part of the Charles A. Lindbergh Home and Visitor Center (1620 S. Lindbergh Dr.; 320.616.5421). It is open for guided tours from Memorial Day through September (Th-Su).

The Minnesota Fishing Museum (304 W. Broadway; 320.616.2011) hosts a fun and eccentric collection of decoys and antique outboard motors, plus displays on the record fish caught around Minnesota. You don't need to be a fishing enthusiast to enjoy a visit.

Guided tours of the Linden Hill Historic Mansions (608 Highland Ave.; 320.616.5580) offer a peek at the lifestyles of the rich and famous. The riverfront homes were built for the children of lumber barons Frederick Weyerhaeuser (his son Charles) and Peter Musser (his son Drew).

Pine Grove Park (on Highway 27 next to the zoo) has fifty-seven acres of old growth red and white pine trees. A walk through the area is a good way to get a sense of what the old growth forests were like.

Little Falls has a good arts scene, including some cool public art. Frank Gosiak painted three murals around town. Two are on the old Hennepin Paper Company Warehouse on Broadway at 1st Street NW; the other is on 2nd Street at Broadway West.

Little Falls native Charles Kapsner painted two frescoes for Lindbergh Elementary School (102 9th St. SE) using traditional 15th century techniques; he learned fresco techniques while studying in Italy. *The Stewardship* is a tribute to the life and work of Charles Lindbergh; it is inside the school but visible 24/7 from the entrance on 9th Street. The other fresco, *Beginnings*, portrays some of central Minnesota's major historical events; you'll need to contact the school for a tour to view it.

In September, Little Falls hosts a very popular Arts and Craft Fair.

If you'd like to get out for a hike or a scenic walk, Crane Meadows National Wildlife Refuge (19502 Irid Rd.; 320.632.1575) is a few miles out of town; a few pairs of sandhill cranes nest in the refuge.

Best For:

The main sites could be visited in a day, but why not stick around a night or two and explore the area? Little Falls has a range of lodging options from camping at Charles Lindbergh State Park (1615 S. Lindbergh Dr.; 320.616.2525) to the Waller House Inn (301 3rd St. SE; 320.632.2836) and the standard chain hotels.

More About Little Falls

For more information about Little Falls, head to MississippiValleyTraveler.com/little-falls/.

STOCKHOLM, WISCONSIN
(66)

Stockholm, WI

When the Peterson brothers left Sweden in 1849, they had no way of knowing that their migration would ultimately lead to the founding of what is arguably the most charming small town along the Upper Mississippi.

In 1849, Eric Peterson and two brothers emigrated to the US. While the brothers went to California to prospect for gold, Eric ended up working in a logging camp in Wisconsin. In 1851, Eric passed through the site of today's village and liked what he saw, so he filed a claim. He sent a letter to another brother, Jakob, encouraging him to emigrate to the US, too. Eric eventually tired of waiting for a reply and went back to Sweden, only to find that Jakob had already left.

Eric didn't waste his time back in Sweden. He got married, then organized emigration for 200 people from his hometown. Eric turned out to be a first-rate cad, though. He booked the cheapest possible quarters on the ship and made the group ride in cattle cars on the train after they reached the US. One-third of the people in his group died while traveling, including his own mother. Of the original two hundred people who left Sweden with Peterson, only thirty made it to his land in Wisconsin. (Some of the survivors opted to stay in Moline, Illinois.)

His brother, Jakob, had a rough go of it, too. The captain of their trans-Atlantic ship died en route, and his son took over. The son wasn't a great captain, as it turned out: he ran the ship into an iceberg before turning south to warmer waters. Jakob also suffered the loss of a daughter during the trip. And you thought flying in coach with your knees in your chest was an ordeal.

The Petersons got their act together well enough to build a few houses and to found the village of Stockholm. It has been a small agricultural village from the start. In the 1870s, Paul Sandquist paid the bills by making lemon beer, while neighbor John Gunderson was known for his spruce beer. As the farm economy changed, the village steadily lost population, but in the 1970s several artists bought property and moved to town. They now form the core of the village's population.

What to Expect

Small shops featuring the work of local artists.

What to Visit

Walk around the compact business district and explore the galleries and shops.

If you can visit in mid-July, go to the Stockholm Art Fair; it's one of the most popular in the region, drawing thousands of daytrippers.

All that shopping and walking around will probably make you hungry, so you might want to grab a slice of pie at The Stockholm Pie Company (N2030 Spring St.; 715.442.5505).

You won't find lemon or spruce beer in Stockholm anymore, but Maiden Rock Winery & Cidery (W12266 King Lane; 715.448.3502) carries on the local brewing tradition with good ciders.

Best For:

A day trip or as a base for a weekend exploring the area. Stockholm has several excellent boutique lodging options, including the Great River B&B (W11976 State Highway 35; 800.657.4756) and Maidenwood Lodge (N447 244th St.; 715.544.7771).

More About Stockholm

For more information about Stockholm, head to MississippiValleyTraveler.com/Stockholm.

PEPIN, WISCONSIN
(837)

Sailing on Lake Pepin

William Boyd Newcomb, a cousin of an early settler named John McCain (not the John McCain you're thinking of) founded a village in 1846 that was first called, appropriately, Newcomb's Landing. Newcomb gave up the glamorous life of a teacher to cut down trees in winter and to pilot riverboats in summer.

In 1855, the village, which was then the seat of county government and heavily reliant on the logging industry, was renamed North Pepin, but the rebranding didn't usher in an economic boom. Within a short time, the county seat was moved to Durand, the area logging boom ended, and low river levels made it increasingly obvious that the town had an unreliable landing for steamboats.

The village seemed fated to fade away, but commercial fishing and a growing local farm economy breathed new life into Pepin. The railroad came through in 1886, which gave the fishing industry access to new markets in New York and the South. Pepin did OK for a couple of generations thanks to those two industries, as well as light manufacturing (pearl buttons, bobsleds, and pickles). As those businesses declined, more folks commuted to work elsewhere, but the village has maintained a strong core. Today, tourism plays a significant part in the village's economy.

What to Expect
Good food and views, with a heavy dose of stories about Laura Ingalls Wilder.

What to Visit

Author Laura Ingalls Wilder was born just outside of Pepin, so the village celebrates its ties to her with the Laura Ingalls Wilder Museum (306 3rd St.; 715.442.2142) and a replica of the cabin where she was born (seven miles out of town on County Road CC). The town's big event is, appropriately enough, Laura Ingalls Wilder Days, which is celebrated in September.

Stop in and visit Smith Brothers Landing on the riverfront (200 E. Marina Dr.; 715.442.2248). Artist Dave Smith's family has been in the area for several generations. He's a good source for local history, as well as cool metal and glass artworks.

You can get on the river even if you don't have a boat of your own; Sail Pepin (400 1st St.; 715.442.4424) runs sailboat tours on Lake Pepin.

For some local flavor, stop in to Paul and Fran's Grocery (410 2nd St.; 715.442.2441) and stock up on homemade sausages.

The Villa Belleza Winery (1420 3rd St.; 715.442.2424) is in the striking Mediterranean-style building on the north end of town; they have a tasting room where you can sample their wines.

Best For:

A day trip or as a base for a weekend exploring the area. Pepin has several boutique lodging options.

More About Pepin

For more information about Pepin, head to mississippivalleytraveler.com/Pepin.

Lake Pepin

Lake Pepin is a twenty-five-thousand-acre natural lake formed by the Chippewa River delta. The Chippewa deposits more silt and sand than the Mississippi can carry away, so a natural dam has formed. The lake is twenty-two miles long and has a maximum width of two-and-a-half miles, with a typical depth between twenty and thirty-two feet. It is a popular place for sailing in summer and ice boating in winter.

Father Louis Hennepin wanted to name it Lake of Tears, maybe because he was captured by Dakota Indians in 1680 near its southern end, but French explorers who did not have the kidnapping experience called it Lac Bon Secours or Lake of Good Hope. Ultimately, the name that stuck is probably derived from Pepin the Short, ruler of France from 740 to 768, who was Charlemagne's father.

Lake Pepin is facing serious environmental threats today, most notably from agricultural runoff carried down the Minnesota River. The latest studies found that ten times the normal amount of silt is being dumped into the lake, a pace that that is filling in shallow side channels and, if it continues unabated, would fill the ten-thousand-year-old lake completely in about three hundred years.

LAKE CITY, MINNESOTA
(5,063)

Lake City, MN

Many of the early settlers in this area came from New England in the 1850s, founding small communities like Florence and Central Point. Lake City eventually won out as the place with the best future, primarily because it had the best steamboat landing (unlike its neighbor across the lake, Pepin, Wisconsin). In 1858, Lake City counted 1,500 steamboat landings. Its population boomed, especially after the Civil War—growing from 300 residents in 1856 to 2,500 in 1870.

The town attracted the usual river-related businesses like clamming, button manufacturing, and grain shipping. When the railroad arrived in 1872, the elevators were moved from the lakefront to the railroad tracks, ending the boom years of river commerce. Still, the town attracted a good retail trade. Farm families from throughout the area did their shopping downtown.

Lake City today is a picturesque community with a big tourism industry. The town's population doubles during the summer, especially on weekends, as visitors flock to the area for lakeside strolls, sailing, and dining out.

What to Expect

A resort town atmosphere mixed with pockets of local culture.

What to Visit

Lake City has a stunning riverfront. The views are best enjoyed with a leisurely walk along the two-and-a-half mile River Walk trail.

Another way to take in the views is with a cruise on the *Pearl of the Lake* (100 Central Point Rd.; 651.345.5188), a replica of a small paddlewheeler.

If you're in the area at the end of June, watch for Waterski Days, which celebrates the popular sport that began right here on Lake Pepin. In 1922, eighteen-year-old Ralph Samuelson strapped two pine boards to his feet and skidded across the water behind a boat piloted by his brother.

If you're out on the water, try to find Pepie, the lake monster whose fame goes back centuries. Depending upon whom you ask, Pepie could be a very large fish, a monster, or a massive stump.

Best For:

A day trip or as a base for a weekend exploring the area. Lake City has a full range of lodging options, including the aptly named Frog & Bear B&B (411 W. Center; 651.345.2764).

More About Lake City

For more information about Lake City, head to MississippiValleyTraveler.com/Lake-City.

The Sea Wing Tragedy

On the morning of July 13, 1890, Captain David Wethern guided the 135-foot *Sea Wing* and an attached barge/dance floor, the *Jim Grant*, from Diamond Bluff, Wisconsin, for a day-long excursion to Lake City and back. He docked at Lake City just before noon and passengers spent the afternoon picnicking and shopping.

It wasn't entirely clear if the weather would cooperate long enough to get them back home. When a break in the rain appeared, passengers boarded and the boat left Lake City. An hour later, a strong burst of wind roared across Lake Pepin so Captain Wethern turned the boat to head into the storm. The boat was no match for the fierce circulating winds, though, which caused the top-heavy boat to capsize. The barge became separated and the 50 people on board floated helplessly away.

Many passengers drowned in the capsized boat, including Nellie and Perley Wethern, the wife and eight-year-old son of the captain. He survived by breaking the glass in the pilot house and swimming out. The 50 people on the barge survived; some swam to shore, but most were rescued after floating around for a while.

The accident killed 98 of the *Sea Wing's* 215 passengers; 77 of the dead were from Red Wing. Perhaps most shocking, 50 of the 57 women on board drowned. Five thousand people attended the memorial service in Red Wing.

While the cause of the accident has never been clear, Captain Wethern received most of the blame (primarily for overloading the boat) and was shunned by the communities along the lake.

WABASHA, MINNESOTA
(2,521)

National Eagle Center

The oldest city in Minnesota, Wabasha traces its roots to the 1820s. Named after Dakota Indian Chief Wabashaw who lived in the area, the early village was a melting pot: French Canadians, Dakota Indians, and English who were later joined by Germans, Irish, and Scandinavians. Lumber and milling were important industries, but many residents also lived off the river by clamming, fishing, harvesting ice, and building boats.

When the railroad connected the city to St. Paul in 1871, it ensured the city's future (while killing the prospects for its neighbor, Reads Landing). Wabasha was big enough that it served as the regional shopping hub for generations, especially for the small farmers in the immediate area.

When the first river bridge was completed in 1931, it was built with an S-ramp that directed traffic right to the business district. The city today still has some light manufacturing, but tourism is increasingly important.

What to Expect

An emphasis on eagles and one of the few riverfronts without railroad tracks.

What to Visit

The Mississippi River at Wabasha usually has open water throughout the winter, which attracts a lot of hungry bald eagles. Even better, because of the recovery in the bald eagle population, there are several eagles who live in the area all year. Wabasha was therefore a good location for the National Eagle Center (50 Pembroke Ave.; 651.565.4989), which has displays about the birds, viewing platforms, and public events that often feature eagles rescued from serious injury. In March, the Eagle Center hosts SOAR with the Eagles, with special events that every weekend.

Wabasha is blessed with an attractive spot on the Mississippi and a maze of backwater channels through the Chippewa River Delta. You can paddle through this area on your own or with local experts from the Broken Paddle Guiding Company (brokenpaddleguiding.com).

Wabasha was the setting for the *Grumpy Old Men* movies with Jack Lemmon and Walter Matthau. The city embraced the fame by throwing an annual festival in honor of the movies called Grumpy Old Men Days. You don't need to be grumpy or old to attend, but it helps if you like ice fishing and have warm clothes—the festival is in February.

Best For:

A day trip or as a base for a weekend exploring the area. Wabasha has several lodging options, none better than the American Eagle Bluff B&B (651.564.0372) and its stunning views of the river.

More About Wabasha

For more information about Wabasha, head to MississippiValleyTraveler.com/Wabasha.

The backwaters around Wabasha are great places to kayak or canoe.

ALMA, WISCONSIN
(781)

Alma, WI

You'd be hard pressed to find a more scenic river town than Alma. The city is basically just two long streets that follow the bluffs for a couple of miles. The earliest Europeans to move here were Swiss, like Victor Probst and John Waecker; they made money by cutting down trees and selling the wood to passing steamboats for fuel. More Swiss immigrants settled in Alma, as well as a few Germans, and the little town came to life.

The first business was probably a tavern, which was probably true for many river towns. Alma also counted a brewery among its early businesses (gotta supply those taverns!). The city won a highly contested election for the county seat in 1860, which added a measure of stability many of its neighbors lacked.

Logging was the biggest local industry, though. Trees harvested from the northern forests came down the Mississippi and Chippewa Rivers to the area, where they were assembled into large rafts at Beef Slough, just north of Alma. Alma had a couple of sawmills of its own, as well as other light manufacturing, including a robust cigar rolling industry. Alma was also the home of famed photographer Gerhard Gesell, a contemporary of Ansel Adams.

What to Expect

A small town with surprises.

What to Visit

Take a stroll along Main Street and tour the small shops.

The view of the Mississippi River from Buena Vista Park is breathtaking and not to be missed. You can drive to the top where there is a parking lot or you can hike up from town from the trailhead at 2nd and Elm.

The Alma Area Historical Society (505 S. 2nd St.; 608.685.6290) has a nice collection of photographs of early 20th century life taken by Gessell, as well as displays on the area's logging history.

You probably wouldn't expect to find a museum on the history of arms and armor in a small Wisconsin river town, but nonetheless, here it is. The Castlerock Museum (402 S. 2nd St.; 608.685.4231) is the brainchild of local son Gary Schlosstein, who began working on this collection when he was ten years old.

If you have time for a meal, check out Pier 4 Café and Smokehouse (600 N. Main St.; 608.685.4964) for delicious, affordable barbeque.

Best For:

A day trip or as a base for a weekend exploring the area. Alma has some good places to stay, like the French-inspired rooms of the Hotel de Ville (612.423.3653) or the Tritsch House B&B (601 S. 2nd St.; 507.450.6573).

More About Alma

For more information about Alma, head to MississippiValleyTraveler.com/Alma.

The Armistice Day Blizzard

The morning of November 11, 1940 was unusually warm, as temperatures reached 60° F along the Upper Mississippi River. It was a perfect day for duck hunting, even if the forecast called for colder temperatures and snow flurries.

In late morning, light rain began to fall, which soon turned to sleet, then, as temperatures plummeted, snow. Winds blew up to 70 miles per hour, creating 5-foot waves on the river. Because of the warm morning, most of the hunters weren't prepared for the rapidly falling temperatures, and their shallow skiffs were no match for the wind and waves. Many were stranded on islands and forced to survive the blizzard on their own; a few drowned trying to get back to shore.

Temperatures fell into the single digits overnight and the storm roared on into the next day, wreaking havoc along a 1,000-mile path through the Midwest. The blizzard dumped 16 inches of snow on Minneapolis and left behind 25-foot high snow drifts in places.

The storm ultimately claimed over 150 lives. In Minnesota, about half of the 49 dead were duck hunters. The Alma Historical Society Museum has a moving display about the blizzard with audio recordings of hunters telling about their experiences.

FOUNTAIN CITY, WISCONSIN
(859)

Fountain City, WI

Thomas Holmes led a group of about a dozen people to this spot in 1839 and founded a community that was first known as Holmes Landing. Just seven years later, Holmes left, apparently feeling like the couple dozen or so people at Fountain City was too much civilization for him. He moved west and eventually founded thirty more communities, including Helena, Montana.

Meanwhile, Holmes Landing became Fountain City, the new name inspired by the natural springs that oozed out of the bluffs (some of which resembled fountains). Fountain City attracted a lot of German and a few Swiss immigrants. For years, all the city officials were German and the language of commerce and at home was German. The city had a variety of small manufacturing plants, including a foundry, a cigar plant, a brickyard, a quarry, and planing mills. There was also a sizeable commercial fishing industry and a boat yard.

Fountain City today still has a strong connection to the river. The Army Corps of Engineers operates a boatyard at the north end of town, and every time the river rises, some of that water creeps up into town. You can't get more connected than that.

What to Expect
A few quirks and cool old saloons.

What to Visit

Elmer's Auto and Toy Museum (W903 Elmers Rd.; 608.687.7221) houses a fascinating collection of old toys, cars, and pedal cars. One of the most unique items is a 1964 Amphicar that was built to drive on land and float on water, a car that would really be handy to drive during periods of high water.

On April 24, 1995, a rock rolled down the bluff and crashed into a house on the north end of town. Thankfully, no one was hurt. The legacy of that rockslide is an odd little museum called the Rock in the House (440 N. Shore; 608.687.3553; open Apr-Oct) that has preserved the house just as it was when the rock made its uninvited entry.

The Monarch Public House (19 N. Main St.; 608.687.4231) is a sprawling, Irish-themed establishment that has housed a bar since the building was completed in 1894. It has retained some original furnishings, including the gorgeous bar.

Merrick State Park (S2965 State Highway 35; 608.687.4936), named in honor of steamboat historian and cub pilot George Merrick, is a nice place to fish or take an easy hike; it also has a quiet campground, with several sites right on the water.

Best For:

A day trip or as a base for a weekend exploring the area. Fountain City has a couple of unique lodging options. You can stay on a working farm at Room to Roam (W656 Veraguth Dr.; 608.687.8575) or one of the bluffside retreats at Hawks View Lodges or Hawks View Cottages (651.293.0803).

More About Fountain City

For more information about Fountain City, head to MississippiValleyTraveler.com/Fountain-City.

TREMPEALEAU, WISCONSIN
(859)

Trempealeau Hotel

The village of Trempealeau stirred to life in the 1840s as Reed's Landing (James Reed was an early settler), a small port and fur trading outpost inhabited by a few migrants from Prairie du Chien and French Canada. In 1856 more people moved into the area and the residents settled on Trempealeau as their village's name.

The name comes from a singular geologic feature just upriver of the town, a conical land mass that is completely surrounded by water. Local Native Americans referred it as "mountain soaking in the water," which French explorers translated as la montagne qui trempe a l'eau. The name was later shortened to its current form.

A commercial district developed rapidly along the riverfront to serve increasing river commerce and burgeoning agriculture in surrounding areas. Speculators noticed the growth and wanted to get in on the action. They bought as much land as they could, which fueled dramatic inflation in land prices and convinced many would-be settlers to skip Trempealeau and move instead to places like Red Wing, Winona, and St. Paul.

After land prices crashed back to reality, Trempealeau faced new challenges as river transportation lost out to railroads and wheat production declined after the Civil War. Even with the arrival of a second railroad line in 1887 the village's economic fortunes changed little.

The town's economic hopes went up in flames in 1888 when a large fire wiped out most of the riverfront commercial district on Front Street (now First Street).

When the town rebuilt its commercial district, new construction was concentrated along the current Main Street, two blocks from the riverfront, reflecting the declining importance of river commerce for the village. This two-block stretch has remained the center of Trempealeau's stable but small population since.

What to Expect

Outdoor fun and ancient history.

What to Visit

Perrot State Park (W26247 Sullivan Rd.; 608.534.6409) is one of the crown jewels of the Mississippi River. Within its 1,270 acres, you'll find a large campground, canoe trails, hiking trails with dramatic views, and the famed Trempealeau Mountain (which is only accessible by boat). The East Brady's Bluff trail is a relatively easy ascent to see the great views from the top of Brady's Bluff.

Trempealeau National Wildlife Refuge (W28488 Refuge Rd.; 608.539.2311) is another beautiful spot to enjoy the outdoors. Its 6,220 acres encompass a varied topography, like sand prairies and bottomland forest with wildlife to match. The refuge has a visitor center, an observation deck overlooking the backwaters, a four-and-a-half mile auto route, and three hiking trails.

The city throws its big party in July, Trempealeau Catfish Days, which comes complete with a parade, fireworks, a fishing tournament, and plenty of catfish.

The Mississippian culture that thrived about nine hundred years ago around St. Louis (centered at Cahokia Mounds) extended their reach up and down the Mississippi. Trempealeau has three platform mounds built by Mississippian cultures; you can view them via a hike along the Little Bluff Mounds Trail (it begins next to the Little Bluff Inn on Main Street).

The Trempealeau Hotel (11332 Main St.; 608.534.6898) has been pleasing diners since 1871; it was one of the few buildings that survived the 1888 fire. Today you can enjoy good food, like their signature Walnut Burger, with good views of the river plus live music.

The Great River State Trail runs twenty-four miles from Onalaska to Trempealeau on a mostly flat route through the floodplain; near Trempealeau, the trail passes a two thousand-year-old Indian mound.

Best For:

A day trip or as a base for a weekend exploring the area. Check out the lodging options available through the Trempealeau Hotel, which include old-school hotel rooms about the restaurant and off-site suites.

More About Trempealeau

For more information about Trempealeau, head to MississippiValleyTraveler.com/Trempealeau.

LANSING, IOWA
(999)

Lansing, IA

Lansing is a consummate river town, with an economy that has, for better or worse, been closely tied to the Mississippi River. Milling was integral to the town's early economy and one of the men who did very well was H.H. Houghton. He made enough money to build a stone mansion on the side of Mt. Hosmer in 1863; it is still there, just above the Blackhawk Bridge.

Lansing was a regional hub for shipping wheat on the Mississippi River in the mid-1800s. Two of the grain warehouses built during that era still stand on the riverfront today. As grain shipping declined, Lansing residents switched to other industries to earn a living, including sawmills, pearl button manufacturing, commercial fishing, and agriculture. Lansing has also had, until recently, some light manufacturing (a button plant just closed in 2016), but tourism is now growing in importance.

What to Expect
Scenic views, down-home dining, and an old-school general store.

What to Visit
Mt. Hosmer Park (enter from N. 6th St.) sits some four hundred forty feet above the river, and it has commanding views of the Mississippi. It was named after Harriet Hosmer, a well-known and somewhat eccentric sculptor from the East who reportedly raced up the hill during a steamboat stop in the 1850s.

Small Mississippi River Towns

One of the old riverfront grain warehouses is now the Museum of River History (60 S. Front St.), which has some interesting displays on the tools and practices of clamming, commercial fishing, and ice harvesting. The museum has limited hours, but you can call in advance to set up a tour (563.538.9229).

Be prepared to leave a trail of bread crumbs as you snake your way through the narrow aisles of merchandise at Horsfalls Lansing Department Store (300 & 360 Main St.; 563.538.4966). The shelves are stacked high with everything you ever imagined you needed, plus a few that you didn't.

The Driftless Area Education and Visitors Center (1944 Columbus Rd.; 563.538.0400), at the far south end of town, is an impressive structure that houses displays on the area's geology and history and has a great view looking upriver toward Lansing.

Best For:

A day trip or as a base for a weekend exploring the area. There are a few boutique lodging options in Lansing, like the 4 rehabbed suites at McGarrity's Inn on Main (203 Main St.; 563.538.9262).

More about Lansing

For more information about Lansing, head to MississippiValleyTraveler.com/Lansing.

The Mississippi River from Mt. Hosmer in Lansing, Iowa.

PRAIRIE DU CHIEN, WISCONSIN
(5,911)

Prairie du Chien, WI

Prairie du Chien is one of the oldest communities along the Mississippi River, with roots deep into the 18th century. Once the site of an annual meeting of fur traders, Native Americans, and merchants, Prairie du Chien now hosts an annual event re-creating that gathering.

It's not clear when the first Europeans built permanent homes in the area, but the village had several hundred residents in 1766 when Jonathan Carver passed by. The town had a largely French Canadian and Native American population for a long time. When George Washington was sworn in as the first U.S. President, there wasn't a single American trader at Prairie du Chien. Most of the residents in the area had closer ties to London than to Washington, DC. That began to change after the War of 1812, when the American government built Fort Crawford to help assert control of the fur trade.

The area gradually attracted new residents, after the American Indian tribes were forced out. Prairie du Chien developed into a grain shipping port and, later, a railroad hub. The original French and mixed-race families were soon joined by Irish, German, and Bohemian immigrants. The railroad was a major employer for decades, but the city has also had (and still has) some light manufacturing.

What to Expect
An old community constantly re-inventing itself.

What to Visit

The original community built on St. Feriole Island, which is now a park. After the 1965 flood—the 40th major flood since 1785—the residents and most of the buildings were moved to higher ground. On the island today, you'll see a few remnants of the original village, like the Dousman Hotel, the Rolette House, and the Gautier House.

The Dousman family built their mansion, Villa Louis (521 N. Villa Louis Rd.; 608.326.2721), on top of an old Indian Mound on St. Feriole Island. Modeled after an Italian Villa, the house was completed in 1868. The house is now a museum and open for public tours. Most of the furnishings are original to the house.

Artist Florence Bird created the Mississippi River Sculpture Park, also on St. Feriole Island along N. Villa Louis Road (www.statuepark.org). She has plans to fill the park with twenty-five sculptures of historical figures from the area. Bird has completed and installed five sculptures so far: Black Hawk (the Meskwaki leader), the Voyageur, Dr. William Beaumont, the Touring Lady, and Emma Big Bear.

The Fort Crawford Museum (717 S. Beaumont Rd.; 608.326.6960) is a good place to learn about the frontier fort, but the most memorable exhibits are those on 19th century medicine, which will leave you feeling grateful that you get medical care in the 21st century.

The Prairie Villa Rendezvous in mid-June draws a big crowd of men and women in leather tights reliving the glory of 18th-century trapper life.

One of best parks along the Mississippi River is just a few miles south of Prairie du Chien—Wyalusing State Park (County Highway X; 608.996.2261). Located at the confluence of the Mississippi and Wisconsin Rivers, the park overlooks the spot where Louis Jolliet and Father Jacques Marquette first caught sight of the Mississippi River on June 17, 1673. The park has a full range of outdoor activities, including hiking, mountain biking, canoeing, and swimming, plus a number of spectacular overlooks and a few Indian burial mounds. Several campsites in the Wisconsin Ridge campground are on the edge of the bluff with great views.

Best For:

You could visit Prairie du Chien for a day trip, but a night or two would be better. There are a range of lodging options from chain motels to cabins and small inns. Check out the Frenchtown Charmer (827 N. Main St.; 608.326.2381), a restored 1825-era farmhouse.

More about Prairie du Chien

For more information about Prairie du Chien, head to MississippiValleyTraveler.com/Prairie-du-Chien.

MARQUETTE & MCGREGOR, IOWA

(375/871)

Marquette, Iowa

I'm cheating by lumping two small towns together into a single entry, but hey, it's my list. These two communities have long had more than a casual link. Heck, Marquette was even known as North McGregor for a while.

Alexander MacGregor started ferry service to Prairie du Chien in 1837, but it was another twenty years before the population began to grow. Early McGregor (the "a" was dropped from the official name) grew largely on the backs of the logging trade: a sawmill, a planing mill, a sash and door factory.

North McGregor grew around the same time because of speculation that a railroad was coming through. The railroad finally arrived in 1864 followed by another a few years later. In 1874, an innovative pontoon bridge allowed trains to cross the Mississippi River between North McGregor and Prairie du Chien. In 1920, residents of North McGregor voted to change the name of their community to Marquette in honor of the early Jesuit priest/explorer.

McGregor, meanwhile, relied on the river for much of its early economy. The town had a busy steamboat stop and several businesses popped up to serve all the people who were coming and going, like hotels and taverns.

The town might have been more prosperous if not for a bitter feud between the MacGregor brothers, Alexander and James. Their inability to agree on who owned what set up a decades-long legal dispute that has clouded some land titles to this day. It even forced Alexander out of his grave. He had been buried on land that was later awarded to his brother; Alexander's body had to be exhumed and reburied in Prairie du Chien.

Both communities today are attractive river towns whose economies rely on a mix of local agriculture and tourism. McGregor has taken a few hits in recent years, first from a steady parade of trucks rumbling through town, and in 2017 from an EF1 tornado that hit the town. Still, McGregor marches on and remains a pleasant place for a visit.

What to Expect
Boutique lodging and charming main streets.

McGregor, Iowa

What to Visit

Just a few miles north of Marquette, Effigy Mounds National Monument (151 State Highway 76; 563.873.3491) preserves hundreds of ceremonial and burial mounds built by early American Indian cultures. Most of the mounds were built between eight hundred and fourteen hundred years ago and many are shaped like animals. You have to hike uphill to get to most of the mounds, but it is worth the effort to see these ancient earthworks and for the incredible views atop the bluffs.

The Marquette Depot Museum (216 Edgar St.; 563.873.1200) packs a lot of information into a small space. Most of the displays highlight the city's railroad history. Take time to flip through the clippings and photos housed in the display cases, which document the pontoon bridge and the many floods that the town's residents have endured.

The McGregor Historical Museum (256 Main St.; 563.873.2221) has the typical of collection of objects and photos that show off the town's history, but they have another set of items that make this museum a must-see: bottles of sand art created in the 19th century by Andrew Clemens. Clemens, who lost his hearing to encephalitis when he was a child, created detailed scenes in bottles using colored sand he harvested from an area bluff. They are remarkable, delicate works of art.

Pikes Peak State Park (32264 Pikes Peak Rd.; 563.873.2341) has some of the best blufftop views in the Upper Mississippi. The overlook above the confluence of the Mississippi and Wisconsin Rivers is an easy walk from the parking lot. It is just south of McGregor off County Highway X56.

As you stroll along Main Street, make sure to visit Paper Moon (206 A St.; 563.873.3357), a quirky bookstore and gift shop, and the River Junction Trading Company (312 & 314 Main St.; 563.873.2387) to pick up that authentic 19th century jacket you've been looking for.

Best For:

You could visit Marquette and McGregor for a day trip, but you'll be happier if you stick around for a night or two. The two towns have several small inns where you'll have a good experience, like the American House Inn (116 Main St.; 563.873.3364) and the Old Jail and Firehouse Guest Suite (212 A St.; 563.873.2759), a studio apartment in a building where the town's lawbreakers were once housed.

More about Marquette and McGregor.

For more information about Marquette, head to MississippiValleyTraveler.com/Marquette; you can learn more about McGregor at MississippiValleyTraveler.com/McGregor.

GUTTENBERG, IOWA
(1,919)

Guttenberg, IA

With a name like Guttenberg, you could probably guess that the town has a strong German sensibility. Guttenberg was built on a plain that is about three miles long and one mile deep. Before German immigrants moved in, this spot was home to a smattering of Europeans and to Sauk and Meskwaki Indians before that.

In the mid-1840s, the Western Settlement Society of Cincinnati bought large tracts of land in the area and steered newly arrived Germans to move there. It worked. Hundreds of Germans moved to the area and built homes and farms. In 1847, the Iowa legislature approved changing the village's name from Prairie la Porte to Guttenberg.

The spelling has been a subject of some controversy, as the German town it is named after spells its name with just one 't'. It seems that the early misspelling was an innocent typo, but it stuck. In 1949, residents even voted down a measure that would have officially made Guttenberg a one 't' town.

Guttenberg's economy relied on local agriculture for generations, but the town also had a large pearl button manufacturing plant, as well as a few breweries and distilleries. Guttenberg today has a nice collection of solid limestone buildings, many of which have been converted to overnight accommodations.

What to Expect
Beautiful limestone buildings and a quiet riverfront.

What to Visit

Guttenberg has a beautiful riverfront that is perfect for a leisurely stroll. The last remaining lockmaster's house on the Upper Mississippi is next to Lock and Dam #10. It now houses a museum that showcases local history, but it is also a time capsule showing off life as it was in 1938. The Lockmaster's Heritage House Museum is open from Memorial Day to Labor Day (563.252.1531).

The Guttenberg Public Library (603 S. 2nd St.; 563.252.3108) has a reproduction of the famous Gutenberg Bible, but it's not your typical copy. It is one of just three hundred that were printed in Leipzig, Germany in 1913.

The town celebrates its heritage in late September with German Fest. The event includes live music, a wiener dog sprint, and beer and brats.

The Clayton Ridge Farm Meat Market (531 S. River Park; 563.252.3820) is a great place to stock up on homemade sausages and other meats smoked in-house. Next door is the Picket Fence Café, which makes the kind of pie that you'll be thinking about long after you've finished eating it.

Best For:

You could visit Guttenber for a day trip or stick around for a weekend and explore the area. There are several small inns in historic buildings where you'll have a good experience, like one of the 19 rooms at The Landing (703 S. River Park Dr.; 563.252.1615) and the 2 suites at the Courthouse Inn (618 S. River Park Dr.; 563.252.1870).

More about Guttenberg

For more information about Guttenberg, head to MississippiValleyTraveler.com/Guttenberg.

POTOSI, WISCONSIN
(688)

Potosi, WI

Once a center for mining in the lead-rich region, Potosi's fortunes have been up and down but seem to be back on the rise today. Beginning in the 1820s, miners poured into the area and set up make-shift communities where they slept and drank when they weren't digging for lead.

Willis St. John was one of the first to prospect legally; he came after the end of the Black Hawk War, when much of the area opened to America settlers. He found a cave full of lead—and snakes, which is why the area was first called Snake Hollow. He made a lot of money from his mine (while avoiding the snakes). Unfortunately, he later lost all his money in a bank collapse and died a pauper.

Others arrived in the 1830s and generally did very well, too. They settled in one of three separate communities in the immediate area—Lafayette, Van Buren, and Snake Hollow. In 1839, these three communities merged into the Village of Potosi, which counted over 1,000 residents by 1840. The boom times didn't last, though. The easy lead had been mined by the end of the 1840s and gold in California attracted many miners west.

Potosi was also hurt by the silting in of Grant Slough, the best access it had to the Mississippi River. Miners cut down most of the trees to dig lead, and the deforested landscape eroded quickly and filled up the slough.

People left town so fast in the 1850s that Potosi dis-incorporated in 1854. The arrival of the railroad in 1884 brought some life back to town (and Potosi incorporated again in 1887), but the village remained a small community based largely around agriculture. Today many residents commute to jobs in other places, but a couple of new businesses, like the renovated brewery, have breathed new life into the town.

What to Expect
Beer and outdoor recreation.

What to Visit
Potosi Point is a half-mile strip of land that juts out into the river from the east bank. The views from that strip of land are spectacular, especially at the end of the peninsula. It's a popular place to fish and to watch birds. To find it, drive south of town to the spot where State Highway 133 turns sharply to the right; go forward instead of following the curve, then go under the railroad trestle, and follow the road for a half-mile until it ends.

The Great River Road Museum of Contemporary Art (101 N. Main St.; 608.763.2440) showcases the works of regional and international artists in an elegantly restored 19th century commercial building.

If you are interested in seeing a few relics from the mining days, take a short walk along The Badger Hut Trail (follow 4th Street south of St. Thomas Church). You'll pass the Old Irish Cemetery and see the ruins of a few badger huts, the compact hillside structures built by miners who stuck around all year. (It was these miners and their unusual form of lodging that gave Wisconsin the nickname The Badger State.)

You should probably start and end your trip at the Potosi Brewery (209 S. Main St.; 608.763.4002). German immigrants Gabriel Hail and John Albrecht founded the Potosi Brewery in 1852, and it churned out popular regional beer until it closed in 1972. Three decades later, a community group created a non-profit foundation that raised enough money to restore and reopen the brewery. That same non-profit still runs it today, donating money to other community groups. The building also houses the National Brewery Museum and the Potosi Brewing Company Transportation Museum. You'll want to save time for a meal and a pint at the brewpub, which can get very busy during the evening and on weekends. Take some time to explore the shops across the street from the brewery, too.

Best For:
Probably best as a day trip. If you want to stay overnight, check out the cabins at Pine Point Lodge (219 S. Main St.; 608.763.2158).

More about Potosi
For more information about Potosi, head to MississippiValleyTraveler.com/Potosi.

GALENA, ILLINOIS
(3,429)

Main Street

Lead mining made Galena, but the arts and tourism gave it a new life. The US government awarded the first official leases for mining in the 1820s, and mining quickly grew into a major industry. In 1823, about four hundred thousand pounds of lead were shipped from Galena; just six years later, Galena shipped thirteen million pounds.

The booming economy drew in thousands of people, like Frederick Dent—the future father-in-law of Ulysses S. Grant—who opened a trading post. Galena was a rough-and-tumble community in those early days, the kind of place that pleased gamblers, drinkers, rivermen, trappers, and other independently-minded sorts.

As the city boomed, it attracted a substantial river trade, which gave Galena direct access to markets up and downriver. It's not obvious today, but the Galena River was once wider and deep enough for Mississippi River steamboats to navigate.

Agriculture gradually grew in importance, too; by 1840 the area counted more farmers than miners. In 1858, Galena counted fourteen thousand residents, many of them quite prosperous and respectable, hardly an independent-minded soul in the bunch. Soon it would all come crashing down, though.

Lead production peaked in the 1850s. The easiest deposits had been mined, so the job became increasingly expensive and labor intensive. Hillsides cleared of trees for mining eroded, sending tons of silt and soil into the Galena River that eventually made the river too shallow for steamboats to navigate. Dunleith (now

East Dubuque) became the terminus for the Illinois Central Railroad, which killed Galena's transportation industries. People began to move away.

Still, Galena would play a critical role in the Civil War. Nine men from the area served as generals in the Union Army, including Ulysses Grant, and the city became an important center for recruiting and training volunteers.

After the Civil War, though, the city's economy did not rebound, as the farm economy supported far fewer people. The city enjoyed a low profile until artists fell in love with the brick buildings and began restoring them in the 1970s, which in turn attracted a steady stream of tourists.

What to Expect
A striking streetscape along Main Street dominated by local shops and good dining.

What to Visit
Walk up and down Main Street. The compact cluster of buildings along Main Street follows the gentle curve of the Galena River and most of those storefronts are occupied by locally-owned businesses.

Galena has several historic houses that you can tour, like the Ulysses S. Grant Home State Historic Site (500 Bouthillier St.; 815.777.0248) with its 19th century Victorian stylings.

For something completely different, tour the Belvedere Mansion (1008 Park Ave.; 815.777.0747) and its eccentric collection of pop culture memorabilia.

The Dowling House (220 Diagonal St.; 815.777.1250) represents the other end of the spectrum. It is the oldest existing house in Galena (it was built in 1826) and has been restored to look like an early 19th century trading post.

The Galena/Jo Daviess History Museum (211 S. Bench St.; 815.777.9129) is a good place to get to know more about the town's history, with some especially good displays on lead mining.

Take a stroll around the West Street Sculpture Park (620 S. West St.) and enjoy the dozen or so playful and often thought-provoking works by artist John Martinson.

The big event of the social season is the Galena Country Fair, which draws thousands of people to town for a busy October weekend focused on arts and crafts.

Best For:
Stay for a night or two. Galena has a wealth of boutique lodging options (219 S. Main St.; 608.763.2158). Go to the link below for a list of my recommendations.

More about Galena
For more information about Galena, head to MississippiValleyTraveler.com/Galena.

BELLEVUE, IOWA
(2,191)

Bellevue, IA

Built on a high bank, the city was named by John Bell, who platted the town in 1835 and summoned his modesty to call it Bell View, which was later altered to its current form. Bellevue is one of a handful of towns that got their initial city charter directly from the US government. Congress passed a bill allowing incorporation in 1835—before Iowa was a state—but no one was going to rush those residents into making any decisions; it took them six years to elect their first Trustees.

Bellevue, like many river towns, sometimes struggled to maintain order. The so-called Bellevue War was the culmination of a local conflict between William Brown, a hotel owner and Justice of the Peace, and William Warren, the Sheriff. Brown was widley believed to be the mastermind of a criminal gang. When he was suspected of committing a couple of petty crimes in April 1840, Sheriff Warren pounced on the opportunity by organizing a posse to arrest him and get him out of town.

Brown heard about the plan, though, and retreated to his hotel with a small group of men. They refused to surrender, so residents fled the town as the posse moved in. The groups fired on each other, then the posse torched the hotel, which put a quick end to the conflict. Seven people died, including Brown, and thirteen more were arrested. The end of the battle attracted a crowd, which screamed for the men to be hanged. Cooler heads prevailed, though. The next day officials opted for the more humane punishment of whipping the men and floating them out of town down the Mississippi River on a skiff.

After a deadly shootout, the rest of the town's history seems rather mundane. As the economy grew in Bellevue, the town attracted a lot of German immigrants. The railroad reached Bellevue in 1872, which gave the town a boost. Even with the railroad, Bellevue maintained a strong connection to the river. In the early 20th century, many residents made their living from harvesting ice off the river, clamming, or working at the pearl button manufacturing plant.

Toward the mid-20th century, the town grew a respectable base of light manufacturing (businesses like an iron foundry, flour mill, and brewery). Bellevue's best-known business was probably Iowa Marine Engine & Launch, which manufactured racing boats. Bellevue today still has some light manufacturing, but tourism is increasingly important.

What to Expect

A beautiful riverfront that includes a business district that still faces the river.

What to Visit

Bellevue has a beautiful riverfront with a paved walking trail and, unlike many river towns, no obstructions from railroad tracks; it's a good place for a leisurely stroll.

Just south of town, Bellevue State Park's Nelson Unit (24668 US Highway 52; 563.872.4019) has hiking trails, a couple of good overlooks of the Mississippi, and a butterfly garden.

Potter's Mill (300 Potter Dr.; 563.872.3838) has been a local landmark since the 1840s. Today it houses a good barbecue restaurant/live music joint called the Flatted Fifth Blues & BBQ and a bed-and-breakfast with three suites.

Many river town throw a big festival, and Bellevue is no exception. The Jackson County Pro Rodeo attracts a big crowd on the third weekend in June.

Best For:

A day trip.

More about Bellevue

For more information about Bellevue, head to MississippiValleyTraveler.com/Bellevue.

LECLAIRE, IOWA
(3,765)

Le Claire, IA

LeClaire is located at the spot where the Mississippi River makes a dramatic turn to the west and at the head of the rapids that the Sauk and Meskwaki Indians called pau-pesha-tuk (agitated water). Its location guaranteed that the village would have a storied river history. For generations, LeClaire was home base for many rapids pilots—men who had mastered the skill of navigating boats through the tricky rapids.

The village is named for Antoine LeClaire, a man who made his name as a translator (he was fluent in at least a dozen American Indian languages, in addition to French, Spanish, and English). LeClaire platted a village here in the 1830s, but it and neighboring Berlin didn't see much action until around 1850 when steamboat traffic picked up and several new industries attracted residents (mills, lime kilns, a quarry, etc.).

The two villages consolidated in 1855, and local leaders had ambitious plans to build a city of twenty thousand people. The city never got anywhere near that big, but, hey, it's good to have goals. The financial panic in 1857 stifled LeClaire. Instead, the place downriver, Davenport, grew to be the big city in the region.

Still, LeClaire had its share of industry. The LeClaire Marine Railway operated a busy boatyard, and LeClaire, like many upper river towns, got a boost from sawmills that processed the trees coming downriver from the northern logging camps. The city also had its share of saloons; no self-respecting river town would do without them! There's an old story that the saloon furthest downriver was called The First

Chance, while the one located furthest upriver was called The Last Chance. That may or may not be true, but it's a good story.

LeClaire today is one part proud old river town mixed with one part bedroom community. Suburban housing tracts surround the old part of the town, whose residents mix and mingle with tourists in the restaurants and bars along the town's main drag, Cody Road.

What to Expect

A busy main street full of temptation.

What to Visit

The Buffalo Bill Museum (199 N. Front St.; 563.289.5580) is jam-packed with memorabilia that is fun to browse, plus it houses the *Lone Star*, a steam-powered paddlewheel towboat that operated on the river for a century.

LeClaire's most popular contemporary attraction is Antique Archeology (115½ Davenport St.; 563.265.3939), the store made famous by Mike Wolfe and Frank Fritz, stars of the reality TV show *American Pickers*.

Drink up (just don't drive if you do)! You can enjoy a pint of craft beer at the Green Tree Brewery (309 N. Cody Rd.; 563.729.1164), a cocktail at the Mississippi River Distilling Company's Cody Road Cocktail House (303 N. Cody Rd.; 563.484.4342), or a glass of wine from the Wide River Winery (106 N. Cody Rd.; 563.289.2509). All places also offer the option of taking their products home.

The social event of the season is Tugfest, an epic tug-of-war that spans the Mississippi River and draws thousands of spectators on both banks. Teams from LeClaire and Port Byron, Illinois, compete to pull a two thousand four hundred-foot-long rope that is stretched across the river, shutting the river to all through traffic for a couple of hours on the second Saturday in August. It's an event with an inherent sense of humor that competitors take very seriously.

Best For:

A day trip.

More about LeClaire

For more information about LeClaire, head to MississippiValleyTraveler.com/LeClaire.

NAUVOO, ILLINOIS
(1,147)

Nauvoo, IL

Nauvoo is a small town with an outsized history, one that attracted idealists who were determined to turn their dreams into reality, where some of those dreams (and dreamers) sparked epic conflicts, especially during the Mormon era. This is a facscinating place to visit, with a multi-layered history and while much of Nauvoo's Mormon history has been preserved (and nicely buffed and polished for public consumption), it takes some digging to explore the rest of Nauvoo's past.

The head of the Des Moines Rapids has been a popular place to live for at least twelve thousand years. Sauk and Meskwaki Indians moved into the region in the 18th century. At the turn of the 19th century, Meskwaki Chief Quashquema led a village at the future site of Nauvoo of several thousand people.

Much of the land was ceded in an 1804 treaty, although the Sauk and Meskwaki retained hunting rights. By the late 1820s, a small community formed that was initially called Venus but soon changed to the more hopeful Commerce.

As Commerce was growing and shrinking, Joseph Smith and his followers, members of the Church of Jesus Christ of Latter-Day Saints (Mormons), were forced out of Missouri. In late 1838, five thousand Mormons sought sanctuary in and around Quincy, Illinois, before relocating to the village of Commerce. In 1840, Joseph Smith renamed the village Nauvoo, which Smith believed was a Hebrew word meaning "a beautiful location, a place of rest."

Dean Klinkenberg

Nauvoo was a utopian community built around Mormon religious ideology that was governed by Smith and a small group of men. While the village of Commerce had never managed to attract more than a couple of hundred residents, Nauvoo counted thousands. Social and cultural institutions were founded, and men served in the village's militia. Within a few years, a grand marble temple was built on a prominent hill, visible for miles up and down the Mississippi River.

All wasn't well, however. Neighbors grew increasingly concerned about the political clout of Nauvoo and the power of its militia. A schism also developed between Smith and a few other leaders over theological issues (like plural marriage). When Smith suppressed a newspaper that published dissenting views, opponents outside of Nauvoo seized on the incident and demanded Smith's arrest.

Smith and his brother, Hyrum, turned themselves in, but the protection promised by the governor was inadequate. On the evening of June 27, 1844, a mob stormed the jail in Carthage where Joseph and Hyrum were locked up, killing them both. Nine men were eventually charged with the murders, but none was convicted.

The leadership of the community passed to Brigham Young, who, under continuing threat from non-Mormon neighbors, decided to abandon Nauvoo and move the whole Mormon community west. The exodus began in February 1846, as hundreds of people crossed the frozen Mississippi River to Iowa before continuing to Utah where they would build a new community.

The Mormons left behind hundreds of homes and businesses. Etienne Cabet, another idealist with big plans, founded a new utopian community in the abandoned structures of Nauvoo, leading his followers across an ocean and up the Mississippi. He and several hundred followers—they called themselves Icarians—built a communal society under Cabet's firm leadership beginning in 1849. Internal dissent would split the community in a few years, though, and most would leave Nauvoo by 1860.

After the Icarians left, German and Swiss immigrants moved in. For fifty years, until World War I, Nauvoo had the largest number of German speakers of any place in Illinois. The new residents transplanted much of their culture, including the grapevines that spawned a robust wine-making business in Nauvoo. In the late 1930s, Oscar Rohde opened a factory in town that produced blue cheese from homogenized cow's milk instead of the sheep's milk that was typically used.

After a couple of generations of distance, a few Mormons came back to Nauvoo. In 1903, the LDS Church bought the Carthage Jail where Joseph and Hyrum Smith were killed. In 1909, the Reorganized Church of Jesus Christ of Latter-day Saints (now called the Community of Christ) started buying up the property that had once belonged to Joseph and Emma Smith. Wholesale preservation efforts took off in the 1960s. Since that time, the LDS Church has bought a thousand acres in Nauvoo and has renovated dozens of buildings.

Nauvoo today draws thousands of Mormon visitors who come to explore the city's past and their connection to it. The steady tourism business has both helped the town financially and irritated some long-time residents who feel that much of Nauvoo's past has been overwhelmed by the efforts of the LDS Church to preserve Mormon history.

Nauvoo's sites may be of greatest interest to Mormons, but even those who are not members of the LDS Church will find the Beautiful City a fascinating place to visit.

What to Expect

Historic sites populated by friendly and enthusiastic Mormon evangelists.

What to Visit

The Weld House Museum (1380 Mulholland St.; 217.453.6590) explores the breadth of Nauvoo's history with exhibits on the Mormon era, the Icarian community, and the Mississippi River; there are also exhibits on farm life and a small town general store.

The Rheinberger House Museum (Nauvoo State Park; 217.453.6590) presents a wide swath of Nauvoo's history, from the Native Americans who lived in the area to Nauvoo's famous blue cheese. The original four-room house was built during the Mormon era, then in 1850, Liechtenstein natives Alois and Margretha Rheinberger purchased it and added on. Alois' vineyard, which started with three acres of Concord grape vines planted in 1851, are still producing grapes today.

The Nauvoo Restoration Area comprises some twenty restored historic properties in the flats near the Mississippi River. The area is often brought to life with actors in period dress demonstrating 19th century crafts, especially during the Pageant season in July and early August. It's part Colonial Williamsburg and part Passion Play.

While almost all Mormons left Nauvoo by 1847, the family of founder Joseph Smith stayed put. They went on to found a sect that is now known as the Community of Christ. That church owns the former home of Joseph Smith in Nauvoo and leads guided tours of the house and associated sites (865 Water St.; 217.453.2246).

Best For:

Probably best as a day trip.

More about Nauvoo

For more information about Nauvoo, head to MississippiValleyTraveler.com/Nauvoo.

GRAFTON, ILLINOIS
(674)

Grafton, IL

Built where the Illinois River meets the Mississippi, Grafton has deep and enduring ties to its rivers. It was a boom town before the Civil War, with hundreds of people—including many German and Irish immigrants—working in nearby quarries, building boats, and catching fish, then partying in the dozen or so saloons in town when they weren't working. Much of the stone they removed was used to build structures in the region, like the Eads Bridge and the Old Cathedral in St. Louis.

The Rippley Boat Company began building ferries, skiffs, and paddlewheelers at the end of the 19th century. They also built a thousand life boats for the military during World War I. The company became the Grafton Boat Works in 1923 and continued the boat-building tradition until they closed in 1978. Grafton had a pearl button manufacturing plant that used mussels harvested from the Illinois River.

Grafton's population stayed steady around a thousand people for a long time, but the 1993 flood took a heavy toll; about a third of the town's pre-flood residents moved away. Grafton today depends heavily on tourism, although there are still a handful of commercial fishermen in the area.

What to Expect
Shops and restaurants busy with weekend daytrippers.

What to Visit

A few miles north of Grafton, eight thousand-acre Pere Marquette State Park (13112 Visitors Ln.; 618.786.3323) has good (and moderately challenging) hiking trails, some of which come with expansive views of the Illinois River Valley. There's also a 1930s-era lodge (618.786.2331) that is a great place to relax and enjoy a drink or meal before retreating to the comfort of a modern room.

Rivers define this region, but there aren't many bridges, so residents rely on a tried and tested mode of transportation: ferries. The seasonal Grafton ferry connects the town to rural St. Charles County, Missouri (for a fee), while just up the Illinois River, the Brussels Ferry connects Illinois's Jersey and Calhoun Counties (for free).

Grafton has many options for dining and drinking, but you won't find a better view than at Aerie's Winery atop the bluff (800 Timber Ridge Dr.; 618.786.7477). The historic Ruebel Hotel (217 E. Main St.; 618.786.2315) has an elegant wood bar that was salvaged from the 1904 World's Fair in St. Louis.

Head a few miles south of Grafton and you can take a step back in time by visiting the small village of Elsah. Tucked tightly into a small valley, you'll feel like you are walking the streets of a 19th-century village.

Best For:

Best as a day trip, but there are lodging options if you want to stay a night, like the awesome lodge at Pere Marquette State Park (618.786.2331).

More about Grafton

For more information about Nauvoo, head to MississippiValleyTraveler.com/Grafton.

Brussels Ferry

KIMMSWICK, MISSOURI
(157)

Kimmswick, MO

Evidence of human cultures in this area goes back at least twelve thousand years, when Clovis-era people hunted mastodons and other creatures. Later American Indians processed salt from the mineral springs around the Mississippi River and Little Rock Creek.

In 1850, Theodore Kimm, a well-off merchant from St. Louis, moved to the area. When the St. Louis & Iron Mountain Railroad was completed in 1858, Kimm saw an opportunity and platted the village the next year.

In less than ten years, the village attracted middle-class St. Louisans, most of them German immigrants, who opened stores, a brewery, mills, a copper shop, and greenhouses that sent fresh flowers up to St. Louis. The town eventually grew to include 1,500 residents. Kimm retired from town building in 1872 when he was sixty-one years old, and he and his wife traveled extensively, taking multiple trips to Europe.

In 1880, Montesano Springs Park opened and quickly became a popular destination for its mineral springs, dance pavilion, merry-go-round, tent shows, and other diversions. Visitors arrived by steamboat and train. It closed in 1918.

Kimmswick was a popular stop on the showboat circuit but as cars replaced steamboats and trains, retail moved to the highways and away from Kimmswick. As old buildings in town fell into disrepair, Lucianna Gladney-Ross used her wealth and influence (her father, Frank Gladney, was one of the founders of 7Up) to shepherd a movement to preserve what was left. In 1970, she began a determined and ultimately successful effort to buy and restore buildings in town.

Kimmswick survived a close call in 1993 when record flooding nearly inundated the town. The village stayed dry thanks to the work of thousands of volunteers and the National Guard who built a temporary levee to hold back the river.

In 2016, the new owners of the *Delta Queen* steamboat moved their corporate office to town. They hope to restore the 90-year-old steamboat and get it back on the Mississippi River for overnight cruising.

Kimmswick today retains its small town feel even as it has become surrounded by miles and miles of subdivisions.

What to Expect

A compact old town with shops and treats.

What to Visit

Shopping and eating. That's mostly what you'll find in Kimmswick. There's a cluster of interesting gift and antique shops around town.

The Blue Owl Inn (6116 2nd St.; 636.464.3128) has been pleasing diners since 1985, especially with their pastries; they are open for lunch only.

As you walk around, check out the historic buildings, some of which were moved to Kimmswick. Besides the Old House, there's the blacksmith shop (1847), the old winery (1859) and the Barbagallo House (1850).

The Kimmswick Historical Society (6000 3rd Ave.; 636.464.8687) maintains several displays on the town's history. The most impressive object in their collection is an old watchmaker's cabinet, whose drawers are still filled with all the objects needed to build or repair a watch.

Just a few miles northwest of Kimmswick, Mastodon State Historic Site (1050 Charles J. Becker Dr.; 636.464.2976) traces the history of the large beasts that once roamed the area. Excavations from a nearby quarry provided the first solid evidence that humans co-existed with and hunted mastodons twelve thousand years ago.

Best For:

A day trip.

More about Kimmswick

For more information about Nauvoo, head to MississippiValleyTraveler.com/Kimmswick.

SAINTE GENEVIEVE, MISSOURI
(4,410)

Amoureux House

One of the oldest communities along the Mississippi River, Sainte Genevieve was founded in the mid-1700s by French speaking farmers. Nearly three centuries later, the center of town still resembles a French colonial village.

Salt deposits around Saline Creek attracted some early interest, but most of the first French Canadians who moved to the area came to farm. Many moved to Sainte Genevieve from other French settlements in the area, like Cahokia, Kaskaskia, and Prairie du Rocher, especially after England gained control of the east bank in 1763.

At the time of Sainte Genevieve's founding, there were no resident American Indians, although Osage Indians occasionally hunted in the area. Late in the 18th century, some American Indians conducted occasional raids on the village, but trading relationships eventually developed around fur that blunted most of the hostility.

The first farmers built on the floodplain about two miles south of the current town site. After a major flood in 1785, most of the fifty residents relocated to the higher ground where the city is today. Residents lived in town while farming long, narrow lots in common fields on the edge of town. Tobacco, maize, and wheat were the most common crops. Forty percent of families owned at least one slave.

Americans began moving to Sainte Genevieve at the end of the 18th century and German Catholics around 1840. For a brief time, Ste. Genevieve had a busy river port for shipping iron ore from the Missouri mines, as well as granite and marble, but the railroad eventually captured that business.

After the Civil War, African Americans settled in the south part of the city. More African Americans arrived in the 1920s to work in lime production. In 1930, three of the new residents were suspected of killing two white men. White vigilantes stormed the black neighborhoods and ordered everyone to leave. Virtually all did. The state sent in the National Guard to restore order, and long-time black residents were invited to come back (but just them). Many returned, but most didn't stay. By 1960, the city's black population had declined from two hundred to just sixteen; it has rebounded somewhat since, now numbering around seventy people.

Sainte Genevieve today has an economy that is largely based on agriculture and lime production. Tourism also plays an important role.

What to Expect

Historic French Colonial architecture and antique shops.

What to Visit

Sainte Genevieve has an impressive collection of French colonial architecture. The most common types of construction were post-on-sill (poteaux sur solle) and post-in-the-ground (poteaux en terre). In both cases, logs were aligned vertically instead of being laid flat like American log cabins of the era.

The Louis Bolduc House (123 S. Main St.; 573.883.3105) was originally built in 1770 in the lowlands but Monsieur Bolduc rebuilt it in the post-on-sill style in its current location in 1792-93. The house has been restored to its late 18th century appearance, and even includes a few furnishings original to the Bolduc family.

In 1824, Felix Vallé purchased this federal style building for use as a trading post. Today it is part of the Vallé State Historic Site (198 Merchant St.; 573.883.7102), which also includes the Bauvais-Amoureux House, one of only 5 remaining post-in-the-ground houses in the US. The Bauvais-Amoureux House dates to 1792. Inside you'll find a diorama of 1832 Sainte Genevieve.

The biggest annual celebration is Jour de Fete (August); it features vendor booths on streets that snake their way around the old town area, as well as live music. La Guiannée is an old French tradition that goes back to Medieval times (or earlier) in which folks dress up in costumes—some of them quite unique—and roam the city's streets on New Year's Eve, singing songs and begging for favors.

One of the few remaining Mississippi River ferries connects Sainte Genevieve with rural Illinois. It's a nice way to get some river time.

Best For:

Probably best as a day trip but there are several small inns in the historic district, like the Inn St. Gemme Beauvias (78 N. Main St.; 573.883.5744).

More about Sainte Genevieve

For more information, head to MississippiValleyTraveler.com/Sainte-Genevieve.

CHESTER, ILLINOIS
(8,586)

Popeye Statue

In 1829, Samuel Smith built a cabin next to the river, opened a small hotel, and began his ferry service, which is why the place was called Smith's Landing for a while. Smith's wife, Jane Thomas, was from Chester, England, which is apparently the source of the town's current name.

Chester's first important product was castor oil, which it produced in large quantities and shipped up and down the Mississippi. Nathan Cole opened a grain mill in 1837. His company was later powered by an electric generator that produced more electricity than it needed, so the company directed the extra power to the city's street lights, making Chester one of the first cities to enjoy the luxury. The company is still operating today as Ardent Mills, part of food giant ConAgra.

The Menard Correctional Center has also provided a steady source of employment; it opened in 1878 and has housed some of the state's most notorious criminals, including John Wayne Gacy.

By the end of the 19th century, the city began expanding away from the riverfront and up to the top of the bluffs. The International Shoe Company built a factory atop the bluff, but the city lost many of its manufacturing jobs in the 1960s.

Popeye creator Elzie Segar was born and raised in Chester; many of the characters from his cartoon strip are based on people he knew in Chester.

What to Expect
All things Popeye and good views of the river.

What to Visit
The Gothic Court House Museum (1 Taylor St.; 618.826.5000, x112) is the only remaining section of the second Randolph County courthouse. It was built in 1864. Its star attraction is the old electric chair from Menard prison, which was last used for an execution in 1938. The fifth floor of the current courthouse has a good view of the Mississippi River and the floodplain; you have to pass through security to get to it.

The Popeye Picnic takes place the weekend after Labor Day and features a grand parade and the unveiling of a new Popeye-themed statue. The original Popeye statue was installed in 1977 in Segar Park next to the Mississippi River bridge. In 2006 the city began a new effort to memorialize other Popeye characters with statues of their own. As of 2017, there are thirteen.

You didn't come all this way to go home empty-handed, so make time to scan the shelves at Spinach Can Collectibles (1001 State St.; 618.826.4567), which has an impressive collection of Popeye-themed merchandise.

Just south of town, the two thousand-acre Turkey Bluffs State Fish and Wildlife Area (4301 S. Lake Dr.; 618.826.2706) has several miles of hiking trails and a good overlook of the river.

If you have time for a detour, the French Creole Pierre Menard Home State Historic Site (4230 Kaskaskia Rd.; 618.859.3031) is worth a visit. It was built in the 1810s for the first Lieutenant Governor of Illinois. It's about a fifteen-minute drive north of Chester.

Best For:
A day trip.

More about Chester
For more information, head to MississippiValleyTraveler.com/Chester.

NEW MADRID, MISSOURI
(3,116)

Mississippi River at New Madrid, Missouri

New Madrid (pronounced MAD-rid) is best known for being at the epicenter of a powerful series of earthquakes, but it is also an old community along the Middle Mississippi. Early French visitors apparently named the area *l'anse a la graisse* (something like greasy bend), reputedly because of the preponderance of bear and bison meat they ate while here. That name didn't stick, though.

Colonel George Morgan founded New Madrid in 1789 at the middle of a dramatic loop made by the Mississippi called the New Madrid Bend (or the Kentucky Bend, if you're on the other bank). The village was founded when the territory was under Spanish rule. US General James Wilkinson, a rival of Morgan who was secretly collaborating with Spain, eventually sabotaged Morgan's efforts, and the few dozen people who tried to create a new village moved on.

The governor of Spanish Louisiana, Estavan Miró, then directed soldiers to the area to build a fort and began encouraging new settlers. Slowly, folks started moving in again; New Madrid counted six hundred residents within a few years. It was a unique place, a French cultural outpost in Spanish territory populated by a significant number of Americans and American Indians.

The site turned out to be less hospitable than early residents expected, though. Disease was common (malaria, probably), and the Mississippi kept eating away at the bank where the town was first built. In just fifteen years, the river carved away the site of three forts and three city streets.

From late 1811 to early 1812, New Madrid was at the center of hundreds of earthquakes that shook and reshaped the region. The three biggest quakes took place on December 16, January 23, and February 7, scaring the hell out of the people who lived there. The shockwaves raced throughout the central and eastern US, with rumblings felt as far away as Washington DC and Natchez, Mississippi.

The first quake destroyed much of the town, forcing survivors to live in tents and other hastily constructed structures. Subsequent quakes convinced many people to leave altogether. It took a long time for the village to bounce back. In 1820, John James Audubon passed through; he wrote: "This almost deserted Village is one of the poorest that is seen on this River bearing a name."

During the Civil War, the critical Battle of Island Ten took place in the Mississippi nearby. (The river eventually swallowed up the island.) New Madrid had just a few hundred residents as the Civil War ended but has grown steadily since, thanks mostly to agriculture, with cotton plantations carved out of the floodplain forests. Many of those fields are now planted with soybeans and corn.

What to Expect

Earthquake history and the northern edge of cotton country.

What to Visit

The New Madrid Historical Museum (1 Main St.; 573.748.5944) has several exhibits about the earthquakes, plus displays on the Civil War. The Higgerson School Historic Site (307 Main St.; 573.748.5716) offers a peak inside an old school.

There's a paved walking trail along the riverfront that comes with great views of the dramatic bend in the river.

The Civil War-era Hunter-Dawson State Historic Site (312 Dawson Rd.; 573.748.5340) is a handsome mansion built by William and Amanda Hunter, wealthy merchants and slave owners. William died of yellow fever before the house was completed, and the family managed to hold on to the property during and after the Civil War. The home still has many original furnishings, a rarity for homes of that era and reason enough to take a tour.

Big Oak Tree State Park (13640 S. Highway 102; 573.649.3149) preserves a relic of the floodplain forest that once dominated this part of the Mississippi Valley. There's a boardwalk trail through a dense hardwood forest that contains some of the oldest and tallest oak trees in the state, and another section dominated by bald cypress trees. You can drive to the park in forty minutes from New Madrid.

Best For:

A day trip.

More about New Madrid

For more information, head to MississippiValleyTraveler.com/New-Madrid.

ROSEDALE, MISSISSIPPI
(1,873)

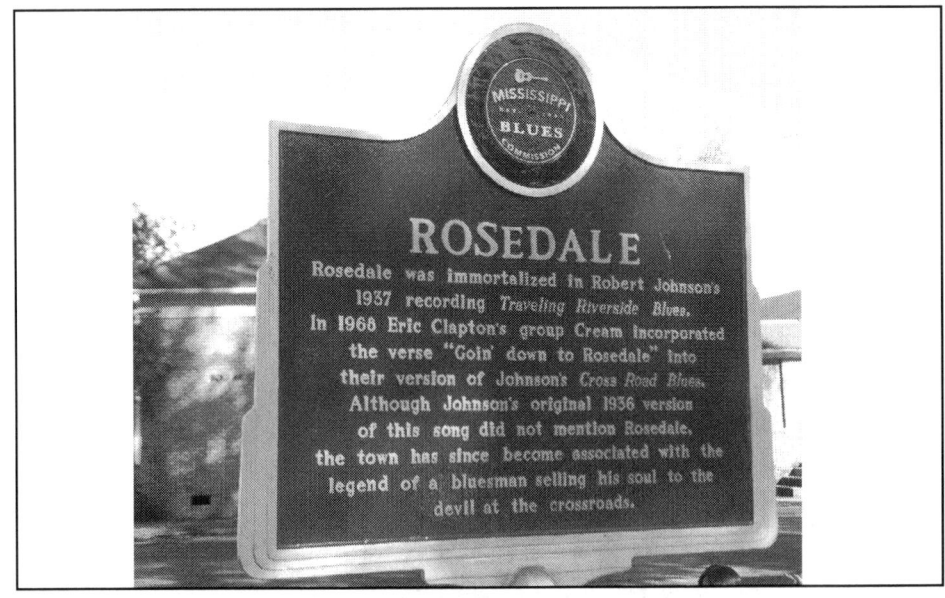

ROSEDALE

Rosedale was immortalized in Robert Johnson's 1937 recording *Traveling Riverside Blues*. In 1968 Eric Clapton's group Cream incorporated the verse "Goin' down to Rosedale" into their version of Johnson's *Cross Road Blues*. Although Johnson's original 1936 version of this song did not mention Rosedale, the town has since become associated with the legend of a bluesman selling his soul to the devil at the crossroads.

Blues Trail marker

Much of the area around Rosedale was dense bottomland forest and swamp well into the 19th century, which is why the city of Rosedale developed later than some of its neighbors in the Mississippi Delta. Colonel Lafayette Jones built a home at nearby Abel's Point that he called Rosedale, in honor of his family's estate in Virginia. The river eventually erased Abel's Point and new developments grew south of there, with cotton plantations as the main industry.

During the Civil War, the area around Rosedale became a refuge for formerly enslaved people after Union forces occupied the area. After the Civil War, the community was called Floreyville, taking its name from a prominent Reconstruction advocate, a name that was doomed to fail. In 1876, the city's name was officially changed to Rosedale.

After the Civil War, cotton farming was still the main industry. Few people had the resources to buy land, so most worked as sharecroppers, which was hardly the path to economic freedom. With few jobs available outside of seasonal farm work, many people eventually moved north and abandoned the region during the Great Migration.

Besides cotton, Rosedale is known for its connection to the Delta's rich musical history. The town gets name-checked in Robert Johnson's *Traveling Riverside Blues* and in Charley Patton's *High Water Everywhere*. Some even claim that Rosedale is the location where Robert Johnson sold his soul to the devil (at the crossroads of state highways 8 and 1).

What to Expect

Blues history and southern cooking.

What to Visit

Rosedale is a good place to get an introduction to the Mississippi Blues Trail (www.msbluestrail.org), if you aren't already familiar with it. There are two markers in town: one about the City of Rosedale (by the courthouse at Dr. Martin Luther King St. and Main St.) and another on those famous Delta tamales (Main St. and Brown St.).

The intersection of Highways 8 and 1 may not look like much today, but this is the spot (some claim) where Robert Johnson sold his soul to the devil in exchange for his amazing guitar skills.

The White Front Café, aka Joe's Hot Tamale Place (920 Main St.; 662.759.3842), is a small place with a big reputation, thanks in large part to owner Barbara Pope (Ms. Barbara). This is one of the best places to sample the Delta's version of a tamale, but don't ask for a side salad; they only serve tamales.

If you snacked on a couple of tamales as an appetizer and are ready for a sit-down meal, Dino's Grocery (1310 Main St.; 662.734.5055) is a good choice. You'll get traditional Southern comfort food and friendly service for a reasonable price.

Great River Road State Park (100 State Park Rd.; 662.759.6762) is one of the few places in the area where it's possible to get near the Mississippi River without trespassing, although it's still very hard to reach the river's edge. The flood of 2011 did a lot of damage, though, and repairs have been slow in coming. Even if you can't get to the river, you can walk through a dense bottomlands forest, and there are many places to fish. The park is officially open during the day Wednesday through Sunday.

Best For:

A day trip, especially if you have time for a hike through Great River Road State Park.

More about Rosedale

For more information about Rosedale, head to visitmississippi.org and search for "Rosedale."

LAKE VILLAGE, ARKANSAS
(2,575)

Lake Village, AR

Chicot County, Arkansas, was organized in 1823, but they had a hard time finding the right spot for a county seat; the Mississippi River destroyed the first two. Vilemont was a typical river town of its day (lots of shady characters) but the river destroyed it in 1847. Columbia was the next county seat, but the river swallowed it up, too. County officials tried out an inland location at the village of Masona, but it was too far removed from river commerce, so they finally settled on Lake Village as the county seat.

Lake Village was founded in 1857 next to five thousand-acre Lake Chicot, an oxbow lake that was part of the main channel of the Mississippi River until about seven hundred years ago. French explorer Robert de La Salle gave the lake its current name in the 17th century. Chicot is a French word for a tree stump; La Salle looked at the cypress knees in the lake and assumed they were all stumps.

Lake Village was home to a popular resort area in early 1900s, but deforestation and cultivation of the surrounding land dramatically increased the amount of silt entering the lake. As the water got muddier and muddier, tourists stopped coming. In 1985 the US Army Corps of Engineers built a pumping facility to divert silt-laden water directly to the Mississippi from the lake. As the lake cleared up, visitors came back. Today it is a popular place to fish and relax.

What to Expect

Fishing, boating, waterskiing, and plenty of time to relax.

What to Visit

The lake is the main draw. The city has plenty of park space along the lakefront; for a longer stay, head to Lake Chicot State Park (2542 State Hwy 257; 870.265.5480) at the north end of the lake (about 8 miles from town). The park has a visitors center that offers ranger-led tours along the levee and on the water. The state park also has a large campground with cabins and a marina where you can rent small boats.

Chicot County RV Park (819 Lakehall Rd.; 870.265.3500) has additional RV and camping sites.

The Greek Revival Lakeport Plantation (601 Highway 142; 870.265.6031) was built in 1859 and is the last remaining pre-Civil War plantation on the Mississippi River in Arkansas. Cotton has been grown continuously since the 1830s at Lakeport. Tours of the site emphasize the agricultural and cultural history of the region from slavery to sharecropping to the Great Migration and modern farming. The plantation is a 20-minute drive from Lake Village.

Don't let yourself be fooled by the exterior. Inside Rhoda's Famous Hot Tamales (714 Saint Mary St.; 670.265.3108), you'll find delicious Southern cuisine, including the tamales that give the place its name. Bring cash.

Best For:

I suppose you could visit as a day trip but wouldn't you rather stay a night and relax, perhaps at one of the cabins in Lake Chicot State Park (2542 State Hwy 257; 870.265.5480)?

More about Lake Village

For more information about Lake Village, head to www.arkansas.com and search for "Lake Village."

ST. FRANCISVILLE, LOUISIANA
(1,765)

Rosedown Plantation

St. Francisville has been around long enough to have once been under Spanish rule, as well as part of a small independent country before joining the United States. The earliest Europeans to settle here arrived in the late 18th century when the territory was still ruled by Spain. It was built on a long narrow ridge that counts as high ground in Louisiana. In 1810, St. Francisville was the capital of the Spanish Republic of West Florida, but a revolt pushed the Spanish out. Residents set up an independent government that lasted all of seventy-four days before it was annexed by the US.

Like many river towns, the area had two distinct personalities. The high ground—St. Francisville—was occupied by the respectable folks and the upper classes (literally). The lowlands along the river, meanwhile—including a village called Bayou Sara, a busy cotton port—were home to everyone else, as well as most of the businesses.

St. Francisville escaped major damage during the Civil War. It's recovery after the Civil War was given a boost by the arrival of Jewish immigrants from Germany. St. Francisville today is a picturesque small town where Spanish moss hangs like ornaments between the restored historic buildings. History had a different fate in mind for Bayou Sara; after repeated flooding and outbreaks of disease, Bayou Sara was returned to the Mississippi River.

What to Expect

Well-preserved 19th century architecture and southern charm.

What to Visit

Stroll around town; the area around Royal and Prosperity Streets is a national historic district. Along these streets, you'll find structures built in styles ranging from Greek Revival (Camilla Leake Barrow House, ca 1810) to Romanesque Revival (Bank of Commerce and Trust, ca. 1910). Along Ferdinand Street, there are bungalows and Eastlake cottages. Grace Episcopal Church (11621 Ferdinand St.) was built in 1858; it survived bombardment from Union gunboats during the Civil War.

The annual Audubon Pilgrimage in March is a great time to tour historic homes and gardens in the area and to hear a few ghost stories.

At Audubon State Historic Site (11788 Highway 965; 225.635.3739) you can tour Oakley Plantation where famed artist and naturalist John James Audubon spent four months in 1821 tutoring Eliza Pirrie, the daughter of James and Lucretia Pirrie. He began many of the drawings for *Birds of America* while in residence at Oakley. (The house is closed for renovations until early 2018, but you can still tour the grounds and the visitor center.)

Rosedown Plantation (12501 Highway 10; 225.635.3332) is a remarkably intact antebellum plantation complex. The Greek Revival house was built in 1835 and expanded ten year later. The remaining three hundred seventy-four acres of the estate offer a look at the life and lifestyles of those who lived there, from the enslaved workers up to the privileged family that owned the place. The plantation is known for its extensive gardens.

During the Civil War, one of the key battles for control of the Mississippi River was fought at Port Hudson. Union troops—thirty thousand of them—descended on the city and began a siege on May 23, 1863. For the next forty-eight days, nealry seven thousand Confederate troops defended the city under increasingly desperate circumstances. When Vicksburg fell on July 4, Major General Franklin Gardner realized that no help was forthcoming, so he arranged a surrender. Four days into the battle, the Union Army brought in the First and Third Louisiana Native Guards, which later became the 73rd and 75th United States Colored Infantry. This was one of the earliest Civil War battles in which African American soldiers fought. The site is now preserved as Port Hudson State Historic Site (236 US Highway 61; 225.654.3775).

Best For:

A day trip is possible, but staying a night or two would be better, preferably at one of the bed-and-breakfasts or small inns.

More about St. Francisville

For more information about St. Francisville, head to stfrancisville.us.

PLAQUEMINE, LOUISIANA
(7,119)

Old Plaquemine Lock

As the Mississippi River reaches southern Louisiana, multiple bayous once cut off from the main channel, many reaching the Gulf of Mexico. One of these was called Plaquemine, which might take its name from the Natchez Indian word for the persimmons that were common here (piakemine or pliakemine).

When the French began moving into the area in the 18th century, they found Chitimacha Indians living around the bayou. Thomas Pipkin recognized the potential value of the location and founded the Town of Iberville in 1819. He started ferry service and opened a tavern, attracting a few like-minded individuals to live there. Most, however, did not survive a yellow fever epidemic. In 1838, the town was renamed Plaquemine and became a busy stop on the steamboat circuit. The river has shifted it channel since the village's founding, so the original town site is now in the river.

Lumber processing was a big business in Plaquemine, especially in the latter part of the 19th century, when the city's population jumped from two thousand in 1880 to nearly five thousand thirty years later. Those mills processed cypress trees from area swamps and wetlands until the 1930s, when there were no more cypress trees left to cut down.

The bayou that attracted early entrepreneurs could also be a pain in the neck. Residents got tired of regular flooding; on the other hand, water in the bayou sometimes ran too low to navigate. Residents eventually convinced the federal government to build a levee and lock at Plaquemine to address those issues. The lock operated from 1909 to 1961.

Small Mississippi River Towns

In 1958, Dow Chemical built a plant near Plaquemine; it is now the largest chemical plant in Louisiana.

What to Expect

A look at river engineering and several historic buildings.

What to Visit

The lock at Plaquemine operated from 1909 to 1961. Its construction served as a prototype for the Panama Canal, and not just because its chief engineer—George Goethals—would later serve as the chief engineer for the Panama Canal. When it opened, it lifted boats fifty-one feet between the bayou and the Mississippi River, which was the highest lift of any freshwater lock at the time. It closed in 1961 when the larger Port Allen lock opened. The lock today has been preserved as Plaquemine Lock State Historic Site (57730 Main St.; 225.687.7158) and is open to visitors. The old lockhouse houses a visitors center and museum.

Bayou Plaquemine Waterfront Park is a lovely place to walk along the bayou, to fish, or just to people watch.

The Iberville Museum (57735 Main St.; 225.687.7197) is housed in the old Iberville Parish Courthouse (built in 1848), which also served as Plaquemine's city hall from 1906 to 1985. You'll find it across the street from the lock.

The city has some interesting buildings, like the Spedale House (Eden at LaBauve Streets) which has a surprisingly mobile history. It was built in 1898 of cypress and shipped by barge to the St. Louis World's Fair in 1904 to show off cypress construction. After the fair, it was shipped back to Plaquemine where it has resided ever since. It is a private home, but you can drive by it.

Plaquemine-based The Last Wilderness Swamp Tours (225.385.9562; lastwildernesstours.com) will take you out for a 2-3 hour nature-focused tour deep into the rich but endangered swamps in the Atchafalaya Basin.

If you'd like to get on the Mississippi River, hop on the Plaquemine-Sunshine Ferry for a ride to the east bank.

Best For:

A day trip.

More about Plaquemine

For more information about Plaquemine, head to www.visitiberville.com.

DONALDSONVILLE, LOUISIANA
(7,436)

River Road African American Museum

When Iberville passed through the area in 1699 (he later founded New Orleans), he found a Chitimacha village where a bayou cut off from the Mississippi for the Gulf of Mexico. The early French visitors therefore named the bayou La Fourche des Chetimaches (the fork of the Chitimachas). The Chitimachas were eventually pushed out (they now live on a reservation near Charenton) and the name of the bayou was shortened to Lafourche.

Acadians (Cajuns) moved to the area around Bayou Lafourche in 1765-66. Around the same time, immigrants from the Canary Islands—Isleños—set up a farming community just down the bayou called Valenzuela. Much of it is now on the site of the Belle Alliance plantation, but descendants of those early Isleños are still in the area.

William Donaldson set up a home and a small village in 1808. He built a steam-powered sawmill, possibly the first in America. In 1825, the legislature voted to move the capitol to Donaldsonville from New Orleans. The town didn't get to enjoy the glory for long. New Orleans interests were slow to remove the functions of state government, and within a few years Baton Rouge supporters captured the capitol from Donaldsonville.

Bayou Lafourche is sometimes called "the longest Main Street in the world" because it cuts through densely populated parts of southern Louisiana. Even though Donaldsonville was built on a patch of high ground, some twenty-five feet about sea level, the bayou regularly flooded surrounding areas. In 1903, the bayou was dammed, cutting it off from the Mississippi. Without a current, the water eventually turned mucky and unhealthy.

Donaldsonville sits in the middle of an agricultural area where sugarcane plantations dominate. Before the Civil War, those plantations relied on thousands of enslaved laborers. The city withstood heavy bombardments from Union gunboats in 1862; it was home to Confederate guerillas who had a habit of shooting at passing Union boats.

Union troops eventually raided the city and burned much of it to the ground; only seven buildings survived. Scars from the Union bombardment are still visible on the old St. Vincent's Orphanage building (now a Catholic school). The Union soldiers left after a month and Confederates moved back in, but the Union Army regained control and built a small fortification called Fort Butler. The fort was built primarily by and manned by African American soldiers.

After the Civil War, Donaldsonville had the state's third largest African American population, as newly freed blacks moved in. In 1868, Pierre Landry was elected mayor, the first African American elected mayor of any US city.

While the city's early commerce came from the Mississippi, when the railroad came through in 1870, Donaldsonville re-oriented to the depot. Mechanization in the farm sector in the 20th century eliminated a lot of jobs, and many African Americans left for the North during the Great Migration in search of better economic opportunities.

The city today relies on a mix of industrial jobs (a nitrogen plant) and agriculture (there are several sugarcane plantations nearby), but it is also looking to attract more tourists. After years of discussion, there is now a plan in the works to reconnect Bayou Lafourche to the Mississippi River.

What to Expect

Historic sites and good bites.

What to Visit

The River Road African American Museum (406 Charles St.; 225.474.5553) is jam-packed with exhibits in a converted Caribbean-style cottage. The museum currently has displays on the influence of black culture on Louisiana cuisine, the first African American mayor in the US, and the influence of jazz musicians who grew up in rural areas, like Louis Armstrong's mentor, King Oliver, who grew up near Donaldsonville.

There's a marker for Fort Butler along Veteran's Boulevard.

The historic district has several buildings worth checking out, like the stout B. Lemann and Brothers Department Store (318 Mississippi St.). The brothers opened their first store around 1836. The current Italianate building opened in 1878; it has an impressive cast-iron gallery. Drive by for a look, but it is currently unoccupied.

In the 19th century, Ascension Catholic Church sold off a plot of land for a Jewish cemetery (at St. Patrick St. and Marchand Dr.); it was the final resting place for many Jews from New Orleans who died from yellow fever after the city's Jewish cemetery filled up. Many prominent local citizens, as well as some Union and Confederate soldiers, are buried at the Ascension Catholic Cemetery (St. Vincnet St. @ Opelousas St.).

Folk artist Alvin Batiste has earned accolades for his drawings and paintings. Check out his work and studio in the back of FramerDave's Frameshop (512 Mississippi St.).

The Grapevine Café and Gallery (211 Railroad Ave.; 225.473.8463) is a popular choice for food influenced by Cajun, Creole, and African traditions, all of it spiced with local art and music. It's a good place to take a break from the heavy, fried foods that are so common in Louisiana.

If you want to burn off a couple of calories, take a walk along the trail on top of the levee.

Best For:
A day trip.

More about Donaldsonville
For more information about Donaldsonville, head to www.donaldsonville-la.gov/visitors/tourist-information.

Thank you for taking the time to read *Small Town Pleasures*. I'd love to hear from you, maybe by reading your review on Amazon or wherever you buy books. It doesn't have to be a thesis, just a few sentences about what you thought. You can also share your thoughts with me directly; send me a note from MississippiValleyTraveler.com/contact.

I like hats

About the Author

Dean Klinkenberg, the Mississippi Valley Traveler, is on a mission to explore the rich history, diverse cultures, and varied ecosystems of the Mississippi River Valley, from the Headwaters in northern Minnesota to the Gulf of Mexico. He's driven over 120,000 miles along the Great River Road, hiked to the tops of bluffs, paddled on the Mississippi River in canoes, and floated in luxury for a few days as a guest lecturer on the *American Queen*. He is the author of the Mississippi Valley Traveler guides and the Frank Dodge mystery series (*Rock Island Lines, Double-Dealing in Dubuque*).

He writes about the history and culture of river towns at MississippiValleyTraveler.com.

You can find out more about the Frank Dodge mysteries at DeanKlinkenberg.com.

Made in the USA
San Bernardino, CA
23 November 2019